THIS BOOK BELONGS TO ...

100%
UNOFFICIAL

First published in Great Britain 2024 by 100% Unofficial,
a part of Farshore

An imprint of HarperCollins*Publishers*
1 London Bridge Street, London SE1 9GF
www.farshore.co.uk

HarperCollins*Publishers*
Macken House, 39/40 Mayor Street Upper,
Dublin 1 D01 C9W8
Ireland

Illustrations by Matt Burgess

This book is an original creation by Farshore
© 2024 Farshore

ISBN 978 0 0086 1695 3
Printed and bound in Romania
1

ONLINE SAFETY FOR YOUNGER FANS

Spending time online is great fun! Here are a few simple rules to help younger
fans stay safe and keep the internet a great place to spend time.

- Never give out your real name – don't use it as your username.
- Never give out any of your personal details.
- Never tell anybody which school you go to or how old you are.
- Never tell anybody your password, except a parent or guardian.
- Be aware that you must be 13 or over to create an account on many sites. Always check
the site policy and ask a parent or guardian for permission before registering.
- Always tell a parent or guardian if something is worrying you.

Stay safe online. Any website addresses listed in this book are correct at the
time of going to print. However, Farshore is not responsible for content hosted by
third parties. Please be aware that online content can be subject to change and
websites can contain content that is unsuitable for children. We advise that
all children are supervised when using the internet.

This book contains FSC™ certified paper and other controlled
sources to ensure responsible forest management.

For more information visit: www.harpercollins.co.uk/green

ROBLOX
ANNUAL 2025

CONTENTS

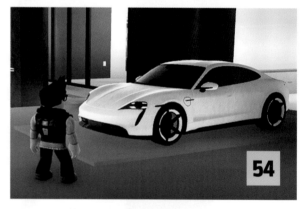

HELLO!

Welcome to the 2025 UNOFFICIAL ROBLOX ANNUAL!

Wow, it has been another incredible year in the world of Roblox! We've been lucky enough to play some epic new games and enjoy our favourite classics!

In fact, there's been so much good stuff to celebrate that we won't be able to fit everything into this awesome annual!

The good news is that we have hand-picked a selection of the greatest games available on Roblox – and we're going to take you on a tour of them all.

Get ready to jump into the cutest pet games, the world of fast sports, titanic tycoon experiences, free-falling obby fun and thrillingly frightful horror games!

We're also bringing you countdowns of the most legendary avatars and best multiplayer games ever!

As always, the most important part of playing Roblox is having fun and expressing yourself! There's never been a better time to get your game loaded, dress your avatars in your favourite outfits and accessories, and get ready to jump into the action.

Are you ready?

Here we go!

TOP 4
PET GAMES

Everyone loves animal games! Whilst these games sadly don't involve real pets, they are the next best thing for the animal-loving gamers of the world. Let's take a look at what you could hatch next!

ADOPT ME

One of the most popular Roblox games ever! This incredible game is all about adopting your own pet, and collecting more legendary creatures! You can also build your dream home and kit it out with anything and everything you want! It's so much fun and super cute!

DINOSAUR ZOO

Dinosaur Zoo Tycoon gives you a platform to build your own enclosure full of amazing prehistoric pets. If you like tycoon, role-playing and adventure games, you can spend hours creating a space to collect your dinosaurs!

PET SIMULATOR X

One of the greatest simulators ever, in PSX you need to collect coins and gems to unlock the game's full potential! Use them to purchase eggs, which will hatch pets, such as the ultra-rare Dominus Egg, and discover new biomes and worlds to explore!

ANIMAL SIMULATOR

This awesome animal experience involves gathering credits to level up and unlock rare skins. You can even roleplay as one of loads of animals. Will you live in a peaceful life in the wild world, or become a ruthless fighter and take on other beasts!

MEEP CITY

If you're all about being social and having fun, then Meep City is a must! Collect as many coins as you can and use them to enjoy fishing, then sell your catches to buy furniture for your house, and play a range of minigames. You can unlock your own Meep to keep as a pet, too!

GACHA ONLINE

Inspired by the Gacha Life and Gacha Club mobile games, this cute town-and-city game is enjoyed by millions of players every day. Create your own character and head off to explore the world, meeting new friends as you go!

Gacha OC

Gacha Online is inspired by Gacha OC, a classic older game. It had a unique style and you could explore the entire world to your heart's desire. There were so many cultures to discover!

Role Play

Gacha Online is all about role playing, too! You can create a whole life and get a job to earn credits and unlock awesome new features. Eat out, exercise, go shopping and meet friends as much as you want!

Design Time

Designing your own character in a game has never been this much fun ... or this difficult to decide on! With billions of outfits available, you will likely spend a long time finalising your vibe. Looking good!

Multiplayer

Like many role-playing games, Gacha Online is famous for its amazing multiplayer fun! You can meet up with your real-world friends, get jobs to earn credits and then spend them travelling around the world together!

Movie Maker

One of the best features in Gacha Online is making movies! That's right, you can make memories with your friends and create custom videos of all of your in-game creations. It's so creative!

TOP TIP

Check out what other players are doing with their Gacha characters and find some cool ideas for sick new looks!

SOUTHWEST FLORIDA

Based on real-life locations, Southwest Florida is a lifelike adventure game that puts the play in role play! Take part in lots of fun mini games or start a job at loads of different places ... or just cause criminal chaos!

Spring into Action

Southwest Florida is set in a world that looks a lot like Bonita Springs – a city in Florida famous for its beaches and parks. In the game, it's full of impressive buildings, places to work and epic highways to drive. But where should you begin?

Law and Disorder

Two of the best ways to start having real fun are by choosing to be a police officer, or deciding to play as a criminal. As police, you race around day and night to stop crimes. As a criminal, you sneak around robbing stores!

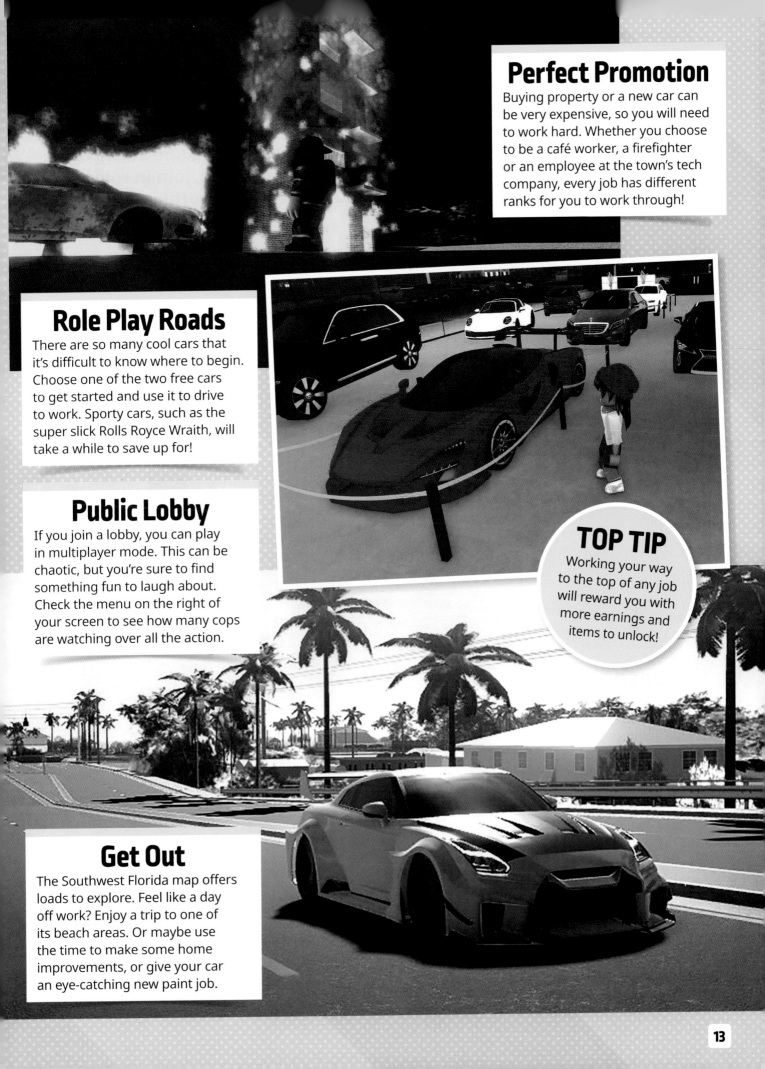

Perfect Promotion

Buying property or a new car can be very expensive, so you will need to work hard. Whether you choose to be a café worker, a firefighter or an employee at the town's tech company, every job has different ranks for you to work through!

Role Play Roads

There are so many cool cars that it's difficult to know where to begin. Choose one of the two free cars to get started and use it to drive to work. Sporty cars, such as the super slick Rolls Royce Wraith, will take a while to save up for!

Public Lobby

If you join a lobby, you can play in multiplayer mode. This can be chaotic, but you're sure to find something fun to laugh about. Check the menu on the right of your screen to see how many cops are watching over all the action.

TOP TIP

Working your way to the top of any job will reward you with more earnings and items to unlock!

Get Out

The Southwest Florida map offers loads to explore. Feel like a day off work? Enjoy a trip to one of its beach areas. Or maybe use the time to make some home improvements, or give your car an eye-catching new paint job.

PIXEL PIECE

All aboard! If you've ever dreamed of heading out to sea and seeing the world, then this is the game for you. Take on challenges, join in raids and explore dungeons as you search for a mysterious mythical fruit.

Open Seas

Pixel Piece is an adventure role-play game that invites you to explore and survive a huge ocean. You will need to sail to discover different islands, which all have a selection of new quests to complete and enemies to do battle with.

Pixel Fruit

Make sure to search islands for pixel fruit, which is sometimes found below trees or in stores. There are three types of pixel fruit, and each will upgrade your abilities in different ways. Pick from paramecia, logia and zoan types!

In Style

There are lots of fighting styles to use, but you need to unlock them as you play, or you won't be able to defeat harder enemies. Upgrade your melee and ranged skills, and you'll soon be a match for the game's most feared bosses!

TOP TIP

Always keep your eyes on the ocean. Look behind you on a regular basis to avoid nasty surprises!

Who Are You?

You begin the game as part of the human race, but you can work towards changing your species. Skypians have wings and can and fly. Onis have +100 health to survive harder battles. What you choose will change how you play!

Boats Away

Your first boat will be categorised as a common vessel and is free to get hold of. The more islands you conquer, the more you can save to buy the elite coffin boat – which is almost six times quicker than the rowing boat you start with.

Island Living

Finding islands isn't hard work, but surviving them might prove to be a bit tricky. Stick with it ... if you manage to defeat every enemy, you can gather their swords and unlock new weapons to buy from each island's unique stores.

THE LANGUAGE OF ROBLOX

Whether you're a newcomer or an experienced expert, there is always something new to learn. You will often notice other players using different words or acronyms to discuss gameplay or status – but what do they all mean?

AOS

If you're playing as police or a law-enforcing character, AOS means ARREST ON SIGHT and is used to inform players of a criminal's status.

AFK

This means you're going to be AWAY FROM KEYBOARD for a while. Other players may describe your status this way.

Bloxxed

If a player is BLOXXED it means they've been defeated in the game and might not be back!

Boosted Ape

Used to describe a player whose level is higher than their visible abilities, so a better player is likely helping them out – or has been.

BRB

If you need to leave a game mid-session, but want to let everyone know, type BRB. BE RIGHT BACK means they'll expect you back.

FFA

If a game has no teams and it is all vs all, it is known as an FFA game – which simply stands for FREE FOR ALL.

GG

Applaud everyone at the end of a game by typing GG, which stands for GOOD GAME.

Noob

This classic term is used to describe a player who is new to the Roblox world and still finding their feet and making mistakes.

Oof

This is used to react to something bad happening. It used to be the sounds of a player being defeated. OOF!

PS

PS stands for a PRIVATE SERVER, which is often the best way to play Roblox games with only your real friends.

Pwned

If you boss a session, beating a team in a multiplayer game, you could say you PWNED them!

Robloxian

This term is used to describe anyone that plays Roblox. Yep, that's right ... you're now a ROBLOXIAN yourself!

SMH

If you can't believe what you've seen, or witnessed a bad in-game decision, you can use this to say SHAKING MY HEAD.

SOZ

There are many ways to say sorry to your friends or teammates, but the easiest way to type a quick apology is SOZ!

TT

If you're coming to the end of a great gaming session, hit TT to say TILL TOMORROW.

XD

Roblox games have a fairly basic chat function, without emojis, so loads of players type XD in place of a laughing emoji.

TOP 5
SPORTS GAMES

Succeeding in the sporting world takes dedication and skill – and sports games on Roblox are no different. But they're not all hard work and high tempo ... loads of them are just really good fun!

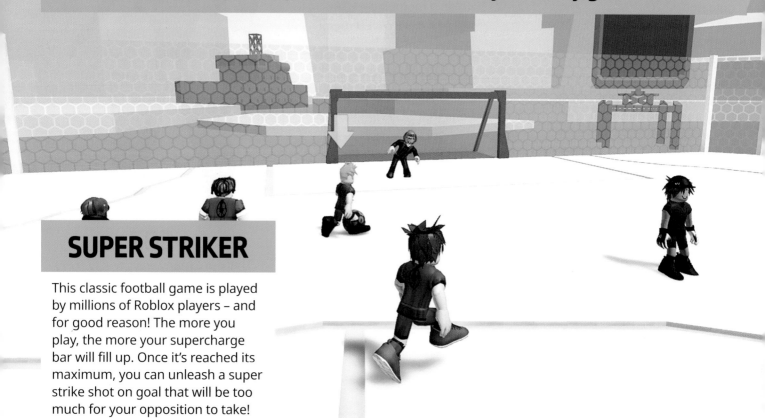

SUPER STRIKER

This classic football game is played by millions of Roblox players – and for good reason! The more you play, the more your supercharge bar will fill up. Once it's reached its maximum, you can unleash a super strike shot on goal that will be too much for your opposition to take!

SUPER GOLF

Just like real golf, your aim here is to get the ball into the hole in as few shots as possible. There are 14 maps to play and loads of different game modes. Our favourite is the racing mode, where all that matters is getting your ball in the hole first!

FOOTBALL FUSION 2

Try your hand at American football in this epic game. Pick your playing position and enter practice mode to master your throwing and catching. Then launch into the action and play as one of loads of teams from famous American cities. Touchdown!

SHRED

This snowboarding game brings all the fun of the mountain into the palm of your hands! You can customise your character skin, unlock new mountains to explore and take on your friends in mad multiplayer race modes!

GOAL KICK SIMULATOR

Build up your power meter and unleash the greatest kicks you've ever seen. Gain in-game money as you kick, and open chests to unlock new balls. How would you get on trying to score a goal ... from the moon? Time to find out!

TOWER OF HELL

This obby game features a tower that is randomly generated to cause complete and utter carnage! Over 22 billion players have tried to make it to the top and beat the world-famous Tower of Hell. Can you do it?

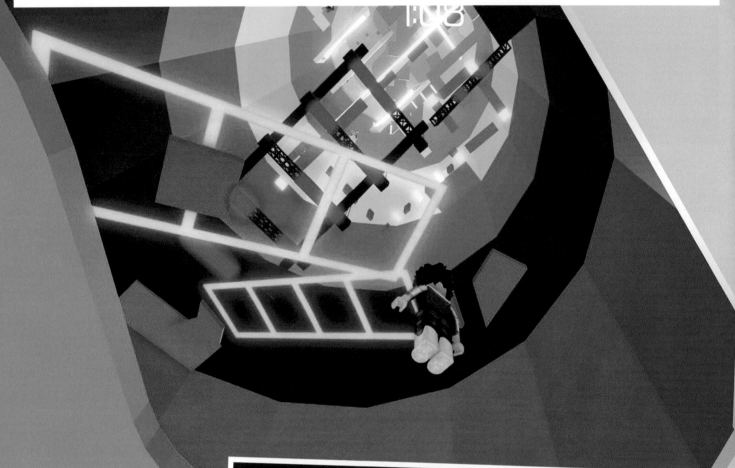

Twisted Towers

Welcome to the best towers in Roblox. They are designed with one aim: to bring you down. Each one is different, so you can never predict what you will face next. One thing's for sure, you'll have fun doing it!

Server Size

Almost 23 billion players have played Tower of Hell since its release in 2018. That's a lot. In fact, it's billions. Unlock your own servers to try towers created by other players. They're totally epic!

Random Fun

The best thing about the towers is just how much fun they can be. Sure, they can be hellish beyond belief, but it's great fun finding out what each one will do in its efforts to stop you from reaching the top!

TOP TIP

Watch and be wise. You can survive for longer if you observe the tower's movements as you play.

Pro Tower

If you're a total master of the game's original towers, then head to the Pro Towers section. These are bigger, better and harder – and are the toughest tower tests you could possibly imagine. Get going!

At the Top

For every player that makes it to the top, the speed of the tower increases bit by bit. This means that if your mates make it up, it'll be even harder for you. So it's in your best interests to beat them to the summit. Let the games begin!

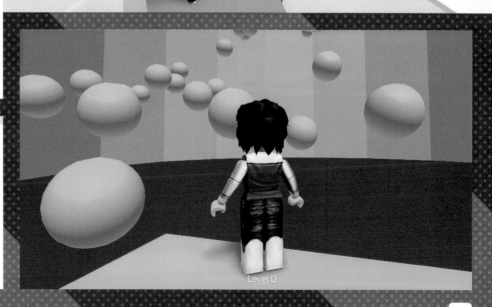

RAINBOW FRIENDS

School trips are loads of fun, but what if your trip turned into a survival game? That's exactly what happens in Rainbow Friends, the creepiest game we've played for ages. Strap in and do whatever it takes to live.

STEP INSIDE THE RING TO PLAY!

2/15
GAME STARTS IN 27 SECONDS

CAUTION

Very Odd World

The school trip was supposed to be to a theme park called Odd World, but you never make it. When your school bus takes a wrong turn and crashes, you are all dragged away to a facility known as Hemlock Woods to try to survive.

Five Nights

As night falls, a mysterious figure releases you into a facility to collect specific items. You've only got one night to find them all and you're not alone. Then, for five nights in a row, you must find items whilst a different Rainbow Friend hunts you.

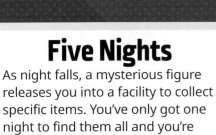

Monster Colours

Lurking in the facility are several monsters called Rainbow Friends. You'll meet Blue first, who chases you. The other monsters have different hunting methods, such as Green, who can find you even if you're hiding inside boxes!

TOP TIP

Try to peek around corners instead of charging around in a rush. You'll spot the Rainbow Friends before they notice you ... If you're lucky.

Safe Sleep

Once you've collected all 24 of the items, you'll return to safety of the holding room. Here, you'll learn the fate of the other players and discover who was caught by the Rainbow Friends. Then a countdown to the next night begins.

TOP TIP

If you make it to Chapter 2's thrilling minecart finale, try to swerve, duck and dodge your way to freedom!

Chapter Game

This game was so popular that creators Roy & Charcle soon set to work on a sequel, known as Rainbow Friends Chapter 2. This amazing addition sees you make your way from the facility to the Odd World theme park itself!

Keep Collecting

If you survive a night in Chapter 1 or complete tasks in Chapter 2, you will receive coins. You can use these to purchase different box skins, which you can then use to hide in every night, as you attempt to avoid being eliminated!

CAUTION

Epic Finale

Anyone skilled enough to make it to the finale of Rainbow Friends Chapter 2 will experience a thrilling ride through Odd World. It wouldn't be a finale if it wasn't difficult, and this level really is a race to survive.

SLAP BATTLES

If you love complete chaos and the satisfying sound of a slap, then this is the game for you. It is fast, fun and totally bonkers, which makes it the perfect game to play if you don't have time for a longer gaming session.

Talk to the Hand

This is a game where you can really let your hand do the talking! The aim is simple: slap other players. Hit them accurately and with power and you'll earn slaps, which can be used to upgrade your abilities.

Love the Glove

You'll begin with a standard glove, which can do plenty of damage! As you earn slaps, you can choose a new glove from over 100 exciting options. There are lots to try, including the Psycho, which glows with a bright light!

TOP TIP
If you're unsure what to do at any time, watch what other players are doing and learn new skills from them!

Power Up

Some gloves are faster, some do more damage and some offer unique abilities that will give you an upper hand in battle. The Retro Glove has three powers: the ban hammer, the bomb and the rocket launcher. It's got so many options!

Slap Battles

There aren't many games that can compete with the simple fun of Slap Battles. Playing with your friends is full of comedy, with comedy sound effects and hilarious slaps. Don't go easy on anyone – even if they're your best mate!

In to Oblivion

The battles all take place on islands that float in the sky, surrounded by a never-ending space known as oblivion. Try not to take damage too close to the islands' edges, as there's a good chance you'll be slapped into oblivion!

TOP 5
TYCOON GAMES

Being a tycoon is all about building a business into a roaring success. Earn currency in your game and you'll be able to expand and create even more money-making businesses. Try these tycoon games out and get to work!

CAR DEALERSHIP TYCOON

This slick game sees you begin a car dealership empire, but it isn't all about selling cars – you get to race them, too. How fun is that? Earn more in-game credit by driving, racing and displaying your favourite vehicles at your dealership. Seatbelts on!

TROPICAL RESORT TYCOON 2

If you've ever dreamed of being the wealthy owner of your own tropical paradise, then listen up! This game involves running your own luxury island, complete with amazing yachts and the coolest sports cars. How perfect will you make your piece of paradise?

ANIMAL TYCOON

This game is all about creating your own successful zoo. Explore incredible habitats to discover new animals and then look after them in your own unique park. You can even craft your own water park for an extra attraction!

LUMBER TYCOON 2

Deforestation is never a good thing ... apart from in this game! Explore Lumberland and collect wood to create your own factory, then build cool furniture and items to trade with other players. How successful will you be? Get chopping!

RESTAURANT TYCOON 2

Who wouldn't love to own their own restaurant? To boss this game, you'll need to pick a restaurant and then kit it out with your own unique vibes and decide on a menu. Can you create something that people will want to return to, and begin your own restaurant empire?

FLICKER

This game is all about solving a mystery! When darkness falls, every player is given a creepy challenge to complete. It could be finding suspects, protecting teammates or even being the villain. Eek!

Night Terrors

You will be randomly assigned to the good team or the evil team. Communicate with your team and keep an open mind as to who the villains could be. If you're the bad guy, then you can use the cover of darkness to complete your task!

Being a Villain

Your job on the evil team can be quite varied. Being the assassin means you must eliminate an opponent, every time the lights flicker, but the assassin can only defeat one opposition player per match. Can they get to you?

The Good Guys

On the good side, you may be tasked as saviour, which means you must rush to revive a defeated player just once. You might be a simple survivor that's just looking to keep breathing until the end. Neither role is risk free!

TOP TIP
New to Flicker? You'll get free hair, shirt and trousers to equip in the avatar editor.

Lethal Locations

Whether it's the sewers, an old hospital, creepy woods, a freaky farmstead or nuclear area, there's a range of scary maps you can vote to play in. Vote for your favourite – you'll know its twists and secrets!

Game Modes

Flicker has three game modes to keep the action alive. In classic mode, you'll operate with just a villain, detective, medic and psychic, while anonymous mode has random character assignments, so you could be given any job!

BEE SWARM SIMULATOR

In this bee-autiful game, you can grow your very own swarm of bees and simulate their real-life behaviour of collecting pollen and making honey. It isn't all sweet, though – you'll have to battle some dangerous bugs!

Swarm and Fuzzy

Get set for the great outdoors! This game is set on a picturesque mountain, where you'll build a hive, then help your bees get to work to produce honey. The more you achieve, the more you'll unlock new areas and fun challenges.

Bee Kind

Your bees will follow you around and gather pollen wherever they can. There are 46 different types of bee to discover, ranging from common to mythic! Your loyal bees will also protect you from any mobs that threaten to cause you harm.

Hive Got an Idea

You'll start out with just a few bees and a small hive to begin quests and earn rewards. The larger your hive grows, the more areas of the mountain you'll unlock to explore. This means different bees and more pollen to collect!

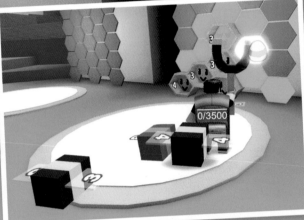

Friendly Bears

If you're lucky, you'll find one of 17 bears across the mountain. Each one will grant you quests, which can be completed to earn rewards. Some will offer you tips and challenges, or even secret codes!

Bee Badges

Bee Swarm Simulator has an achievement system that rewards you with badges. If you spend time collecting pollen from a particular field, you will earn a badge. Many of these badges unlock rewards, such as greater resources!

CREATURES OF SONARIA

Creatures of Sonaria takes you on an immersive survival journey. Start with weak newborn creatures and raise them into strong and lethal beasts capable of surviving anything the elements throw at them!

Creature Comfort

Your main aim is to collect and grow your creatures. There are many different types, ranging from common terrestrials, to fliers, gliders and aquatic types! You will see these amazing beasts everywhere around the huge map.

TOP TIP
Edible plants are one of the easiest sources of food in the game, as well as water to drink.

Food's Good

Creatures need to eat and finding them food is one of the most important parts of the game. By working out what their preferred diet consists of, you can guide your creatures to their next meal.

Key Shelter

Sonaria's elements can be brutal, so finding your creatures somewhere safe to shelter is vital. It'll help restore their energy levels and prepare them for a new day, so they'll be ready to begin all of the amazing adventures that await!

Immersive World

Sonaria is possibly the most impressive world ever seen in Roblox. It's only one island, but it's enormous and has many different biomes to explore. There are also huge bodies of water that contain loads of hidden secrets.

Advanced Creatures

There are lots of different categories of creature to collect, but most of them are difficult to find. Mission creatures can be unlocked when you unexpectedly complete hidden missions that you find across the world. Cool!

Stats Alright

Levelling up your creatures is one of the most important parts of the gameplay. Keep a close eye on them and monitor all of their key elements, such as their thirst and hunger condition. Healthy creatures will level up quicker!

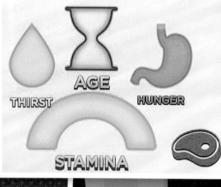

THIRST   AGE   HUNGER

STAMINA

Extreme Conditions

The tundra is made up of many mountains that are sometimes covered in snow, with floating rocks surrounding its peak. It can be found just west, south and east of the hot springs. Surviving here is an impressive feat!

Epic Disaster

The volcano biome is normally dormant and inactive, but if you hear dramatic music begin to play then you should take cover. Molten lava will spurt and meteors of terror will illuminate the sky!

TOP TIP
Use shelter to better protect your creatures from natural disasters and damage from other creatures!

Multiplayer

Creatures of Sonaria is great to play on your own, but even better together! Occasionally, there are limited time events for you to play. Complete these and you will be rewarded with special items, such as the Yellow Bandito Mask!

Progression

Spend your time exploring, feeding your creatures – and unlocking more of them – and you will soon feel like a master of Sonaria. You can either focus on one creature, or collect as many as you can and care for them all. So much fun!

TOP 10
ROBLOX AVATARS

Every time you launch a Roblox game, you play as a character, known as an avatar. Lots of players have their own unique avatars and some games come with fun characters of their own. Here are 10 of the very best!

PET SIMULATOR X

This mega game might be all about what pets you can hatch and collect, but we love looking cool with this original avatar. You'll look so slick as your pets follow behind you as you walk around the different zones. We want more!

ALL OF US ARE DEAD

The end of the world as we know it is less frightening in this epic FPS game. As a school student, you must survive waves of zombies dressed in your school uniform and PE kit for school sports!

WORK AT A PIZZA PLACE

One of the all-time great Roblox games, Work At A Pizza Place offers stylish costumes that reek of fast food! We'd wear anything if it meant we could stand and smell fresh pizza all day long!

BE A PARKOUR NINJA

This PVP game is all about taking on other players in epic ninja battles. Your slick avatar will come complete with two weapons and one special utility, such as increasing your max health or your movement speed. Looking fearless!

BROOKHAVEN

The ultimate role-play game needs to let you express yourself and Brookhaven doesn't disappoint. You can choose loads of outfits to suit your house, job, car or even just your mood. It is a creative city with endless avatar customisation!

UNOFFICIAL

It's essential to keep a straight face as you bluff your way through this popular card game. Your avatar needs to be sensible, hard to read and LOADS of fun – so get creative to throw off your opponents!

PIGGY

Escaping these rampaging pigs isn't easy, but you're looking good! You can unlock loads of different skins, from Piggy itself, a soldier or just a cool kid like you. They look great, but won't help you survive!

SHRED

There's no greater feeling than racing down a mountain on your snowboard ... as long as you're dressed in the right attire! Your shred avatar will need goggles, a warm beanie, thick gloves and all the right gear to survive the snow and make it down all of the mountains in this game. You'll look ice cool!

ANIME FIGHTING SIMULATOR

You need to dress to survive in this epic brawler that pits awesome anime skins against other players. You can even decorate your swords with different skins to make them shine in battle. So sharp!

EXPEDITION ANTARCTICA

Surviving the expedition from base camp to the south pole isn't easy. Looking cool is though, with all the epic gear available. Make sure you are practical, as the elements will do their best to end your journey!

BROOKHAVEN

One of the most popular Roblox games ever, players return year after year to jump back into their Brookhaven worlds. With so much to do, there's never been a better time to start ravin' about Brookhaven!

All About You

Begin the game by making your avatar. Pick a face, some clothes and a name (avoid using your real full name). You can make changes to your avatar any time, so it doesn't need to be perfect now.

Work Is Fun

Brookhaven could be called a virtual reality game, because you get to live an entire virtual life. Get a job and you'll be able to buy a home, a vehicle and items. You could try your hand at farming, driving or working at a hospital!

X - RAY

TOP TIP

Due to Brookhaven's popularity, there are similar games across Roblox. If you want the original version, look for the one created by Wolfpaq.

Dogwood Parkland

Home Time

The more you work, the more you can afford to build. There are loads of free homes to construct, so you can get your own house early. Save money to build new improvements. Did someone say swimming pool? We'd dive right in to that idea!

Making Friends

One reason Brookhaven is so popular is that it gets even better when you play it with your friends! You can work with them, travel and explore together and even have the best sleepovers in your very own dream house.

Flavors

Chocolate   Birthday Cake   Mint Chip
Vanilla   Bubble Gum

Mint Chip

Gum

Milkshake

TOP TIP
There's no right or wrong way to build your Brookhaven life. Make sure you do whatever you want, when you want!

Top Secret

There's so much in Brookhaven that you might not see everything – especially because some locations are secret. We recommend trying to find the location of the dark scary house or awesome arcade.

Ride On

You can drive so many vehicles around Brookhaven. Some are sporty, such as the classic convertible, but others are suited to whatever job you have, such as the police car. But you may just want to zoom around on a moped!

EVADE

This game is all about surviving at any cost. You'll find loads of maps to explore but, unfortunately, there are also lots of Nextbots chasing you. They might look friendly, but stay away from them. You've been warned!

Try To Survive

The aim is to survive for as long as you can. How? By any means possible. Explore the maps while avoiding the scary enemies that are trying to bring your game to an end. Run, climb, hide and try to find a way to evade them!

Nextbots

It won't take you long to realise what is chasing you. The Nextbots are a terrifying group of bots that have one single ambition: to eliminate every player. These destructors won't rest until they do!

Teamwork

You'll encounter other players while trying to survive. It's a good job they aren't all evil, too. Your best bet is to work with others. Sure, you want to beat them and survive, but teaming up is the best way to play!

TOP TIP

If you're unsure what to do at any time, watch other players and learn new skills from them!

Mad Modes

Evade features different game modes, so there are always fun scares to be had. From casual rounds and team death matches, to pro servers and even modes that let YOU play as a Nextbot. What a plot twist!

Express Yourself

Perform a sick move or escape a Nextbot (at the expense of another player) and you can bust out some emotes. Also known as taunts, you can celebrate your skills and wind up other players with a quick click of a button!

Map Attack

Mastering the levels might look like an easy job, but there are over 40 available, from art exhibits to underground facilities. As there are so many, you may not encounter the same map twice, making teamwork even more important.

Neighborhood

Tudor Manor

Mayday

Catacombs

HORROR GAMES

Would you care for a scare? We sure would – and that's why we're bringing you this list of the top horror games on Roblox! You'll need all of your gaming experience to survive these frightfully awesome games!

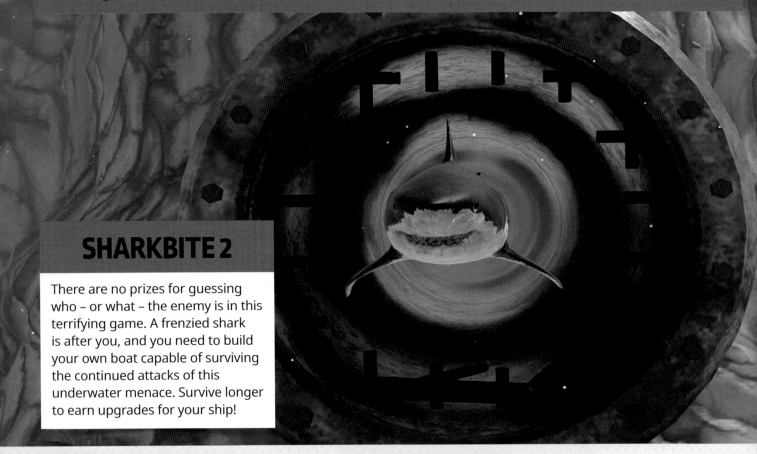

SHARKBITE 2

There are no prizes for guessing who – or what – the enemy is in this terrifying game. A frenzied shark is after you, and you need to build your own boat capable of surviving the continued attacks of this underwater menace. Survive longer to earn upgrades for your ship!

3008

Is there anything scarier than being trapped in a closed furniture store at night? Nope! In 3008, you must spend the night in a huge store that has frights around every corner ... and some enraged employees. Will you find a safe place to survive?

THE MAZE

If you're looking for a scare and like to explore terrifying worlds, then jump into The Maze. Once you enter the walls of the maze, everything gets a little bit tighter and a lot scarier. Have you got the guts to turn the next corner?

CHEESE ESCAPE

There's a rat on the loose and it wants to catch you – and eat you – before you find a way out of a huge cheese maze! Collect all nine cheeses and at least three keys to unlock the metal door and get away from the ravenous rodent!

NEXTBOTS

There may be a few Nextbot games, but they've all got one thing in common – legging it for dear life from terrifying bots who'll stop at nothing to catch you. Explore, hide and survive as long as you can without getting caught by one of these monstrosities.

ANIME STORY

With a combination of anime fun and amazing adventure, Anime Story has been played 19.2 million times! You can shape your character however you choose and create a story that will be told for generations ...

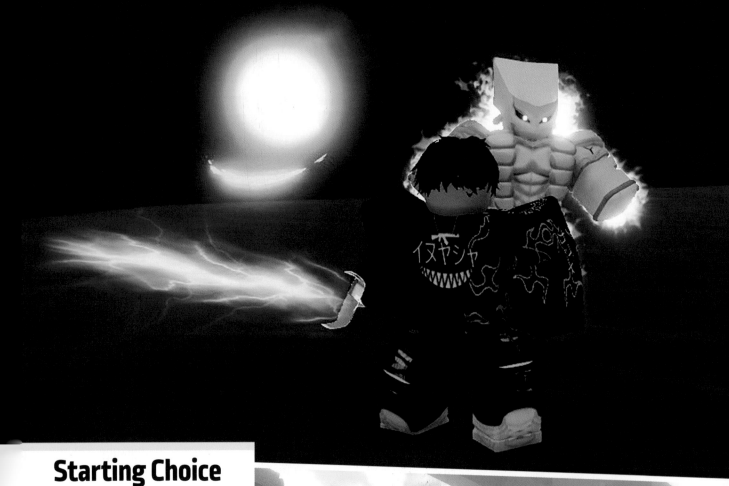

Starting Choice

When you first spawn ,you will have the option of being a hero or a villain. Both are great fun! Once you've chosen, you'll also receive a free teleportation technique – and yes, it is as fun as it sounds!

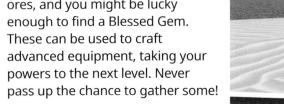

Ore-some

You'll need to go out mining for ores, and you might be lucky enough to find a Blessed Gem. These can be used to craft advanced equipment, taking your powers to the next level. Never pass up the chance to gather some!

Love to Loot

Looting is a big part of this game. The more you loot, the more you can develop your character and progress. New loot spawns on the map every 10 minutes, so there's always something to find.

Ranked PVP

If you think you've achieved greatness and become a real anime hero, then why not take your skills to an online game. Here, you can face-off against other players and see where you rank in the online world of Anime Story!

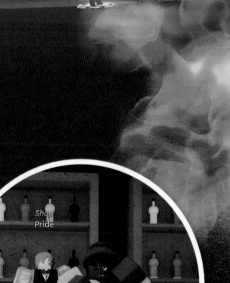

Get Crafty

Speak to the blacksmith near the spawn point and they will help you craft items. As a beginner, you'll only be able to craft level 1 items, but come back later on and there will be loads more options to transform your game!

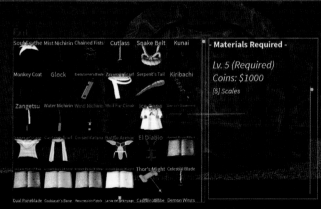

- Materials Required -

Lv. 5 (Required)
Coins: $1000
[5] Scales

Snake Belt

Common | Equipment

A purple robe belt made from snake material, fashionable and defensive.

Health: 50
Energy: 25
Damage Boost: x1
Speed Boost: 2
Tradable: N/A

Craft

PLATES OF FATE: REMASTERED

This arcade-style game throws players into an arena of pure trouble and the only goal is to survive. Walk, run, jump or do anything possible to be the last player standing against the dreaded plates of fate!

Jump In

Plates of Fate: Remastered is an obby game that is all about survival. You start the game on your own plate in a huge arena, and every player is faced with different challenges to survive. Will you make it to the final few?

Dodging Dangers

Fate will throw lots of dangers at you and you'll never know what is coming. It could be your plate moving or changing size, or surviving being hit by damaging lightning or lasers from a deadly disco ball. LOL!

Challenging Effects

Some effects make it a lot easier to fall from your plate! The hottest one is Lava Floor ... which needs no explanation! The most out-of-this-world effect is the UFO event, which triggers an alien invasion!

Total Teamwork

The only thing more exciting than surviving on your own, is surviving with a team! Plate vs Plate or Team Plates rounds are loads of fun. Use your teammates' unlocks and abilities to your own advantage to help you achieve the win!

Badges

Survive or complete challenges and you could earn one of 143 badges! One of the hardest is 1st Badge, which you get for finishing a round in first place – something only 2.2% of players achieve. That's epic!

MEGA MANSION TYCOON

This game has gained fans around the Roblox world thanks to all its features, meaning there is always something to do. You can race cars, visit other players' houses and build the biggest mansions anywhere in Roblox.

Build Well

There's so much to do in this game that it can be difficult to know where to begin! Follow all the prompts on the ground to build your first house, starting with walls then adding the windows, floors and more!

Gather Resources

Building isn't free and you will soon find your money is running low. You earn more currency by playing the game and building, so always check the post box at the edge of your plot of land – it will soon add up!

Be a Tycoon

Being a top tycoon is all about having fun as you build up your earnings, possessions and property. From the moment you start playing, you need to work to earn more in-game currency to spend on anything you want!

Couch
$13,230

Get Racing

Don't get bogged down with building when there's lots more to do. You can buy cars and hit the road to race your friends, but a personal parking space at your mansion won't come cheap!

Secret Island

As your empire expands, you will be able to build bigger and better houses in different locations. There is even a beach house in the exclusive Malibu Shores location or a secret island accessible only by boat – or jet ski. So much fun!

Upgrades

Mega Mansion Tycoon is regularly updated. If it's been a while since you played, there could be new stuff to find. Get online and check!

TOP 5
OBBY GAMES

You need to walk, run, jump and be brave to beat some of these obby games. They're all assault courses that will test your Roblox skills to the limit – will you manage to beat the courses and conquer these obbys?

SPEED RUN 4

If you want fast-paced fun with a real challenge, then this is the obby game for you. It has over 30 levels that you must parkour through and each one has a different theme and soundtrack. It doesn't get much more immersive than this!

THE FLOOR IS LAVA!

This obby survival game brings your worst nightmare to life: lava. You must evade the rising lava and work your way across countless maps, navigating the courses that are designed to send you for a dip – a very hot bath indeed!

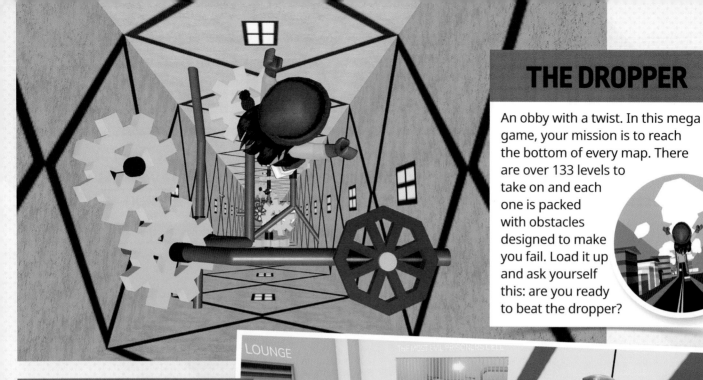

THE DROPPER

An obby with a twist. In this mega game, your mission is to reach the bottom of every map. There are over 133 levels to take on and each one is packed with obstacles designed to make you fail. Load it up and ask yourself this: are you ready to beat the dropper?

BARRY'S PRISON RUN 4

Escaping from prison can't be easy, but has it ever been this hard? Over 25 obstacles stand between you and freedom, and Barry the prison guard is intent on stopping you. You can switch to hard mode for an even more difficult challenge!

OBBY CREATOR

Express yourself and your inner architect in this obby creator, giving you the tools to make your own obby courses. You can spend time building the toughest obby imaginable, or try out the millions of obbys created by other Roblox players. Which is your favourite?

MURDER MYSTERY 2

You'll need your wits about you to survive this hugely popular horror game. Can you trust your team and try to stick with innocent players as you investigate the mystery, or will you find yourself to be the next victim?

Your Roles

Each game starts with 12 different players and every is spawned with a different role. 10 of you will be innocents, but one will be the villain and one will be the sheriff. The roles are selected at random and kept a secret!

The Town Sheriff

The sheriff is the only player that has a weapon, which they can use to protect innocents. If the sheriff is killed (either by shooting an innocent or being defeated), the gun will drop, allowing any eager innocents to pick it up.

TOP TIP
Watch every other player's behaviour and you might spot some clues about their role!

Look For Clues

It is the job of the 10 innocents to keep their eyes open and spot any suspicious behaviour by the potential murderer. Other than that? Well, it would be wise not to be too relaxed and risk being their next victim. Stay alert!

Sharp Approach

The villain is the only player with a weapon, which can be used to defeat the innocents and the sheriff. They must stealthily defeat all the innocents and the sheriff before the time runs out.

Game Modes

There is more than one map to play as the action unfolds. They all differ and offer new and exciting ways to explore and evade the murderer. Master these maps and you might discover secrets for survival.

FASHION FAMOUS

Take to the catwalk and strut your stylish stuff with this super good-looking fashion game. You can customise every part of your look as you attempt to wow the judges and get the highest scores!

Famous Fashion

If you love expressing yourself through fashion, then get ready to be creative! This game is all about crafting outfits before the countdown finishes. When it does, everyone else will take turns judging what you've made!

Get Stylish

In every round, you'll be given a new theme and must choose from a selection of hairstyles, colours, clothes, different faces and loads of sweet accessories. Remember what the theme is and make fast choices that will work with it!

Adding Accessories

Different accessories can be used to transform your outfits. For instance, if the category is Snow Angels, you could use white wings. Explore different rooms to find other accessories to use!

Category Mix

Every round has a different category, which is decided at the beginning. Some are out of this world, such as Area 51 aliens, but others are as simple as I'm So Fancy or I'm A Tourist. You never know what is coming next!

The Voting

When time runs out, players will be whisked to the catwalk to show off their creations. You'll watch as each player walks the catwalk and must score each one out of five stars. You decide who wins each round!

DOORS

Welcome to the hotel of nightmares. There is no way out and your only way of surviving is to reach door 100. This is easier said than done ... because you're being chased by creepy entities who want you defeated!

Ghouls Galore

There are so many ghouls – known as entities – that are desperate to scare you! They'll wait for just the right second to deliver the most frightening moments we've ever encountered in a Roblox game. Keep on the lookout!

In The Rooms

The puzzles inside each room are randomly generated, so change every time you play. You'll need to interact with all the furniture to solve the puzzles and hide from any ghouls that are tracking you down.

TOP TIP

Try to play using headphones. You'll need to listen carefully to hear any hidden entities approaching your position!

Take Cover

One of the only ways to stay safe from the entities and survive the room is by using everything available to you to hide. Enter wardrobes and try to find keys to open any locked doors and secret passages you come across.

Haunted Hotel

The action all takes place on one floor of a hotel. What happened at this hotel to make it so haunted? You're sure to find out as you explore the corridors and work your way from room to room.

Floor 2

Thanks to the success of Doors, its creators created a second game, Floor 2. It's hard not to be excited and terrified at the idea of surviving on another floor of this creepy hotel of horrors!

TOP 10
MULTIPLAYER GAMES

Playing on your own is one thing, but playing with friends takes your gaming experience to a whole new level of fun. Whether you're working as a team or battling against each other – multiplayer is magnificent!

JAILBREAK

This classic Roblox game is one of the best! Play as a criminal and you must cause chaos and escape the confines of prison. Play as the police and you must return the criminals to jail. It's so fun, especially when you're playing against your pals!

OUTLASTER

Elect captains, select teams and try to survive in this challenging game. The objective is simple: take part in minigames and compete to not be voted out by other players! You'll need to work together, or against each other!

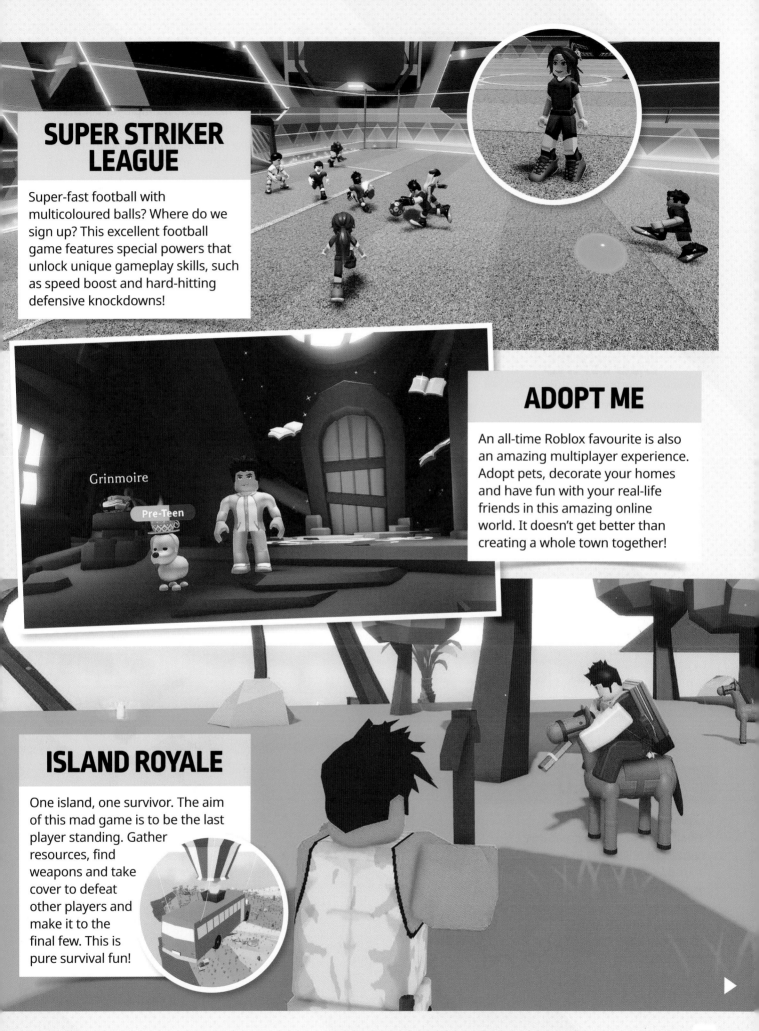

SUPER STRIKER LEAGUE

Super-fast football with multicoloured balls? Where do we sign up? This excellent football game features special powers that unlock unique gameplay skills, such as speed boost and hard-hitting defensive knockdowns!

ADOPT ME

An all-time Roblox favourite is also an amazing multiplayer experience. Adopt pets, decorate your homes and have fun with your real-life friends in this amazing online world. It doesn't get better than creating a whole town together!

ISLAND ROYALE

One island, one survivor. The aim of this mad game is to be the last player standing. Gather resources, find weapons and take cover to defeat other players and make it to the final few. This is pure survival fun!

SLAP BATTLES

This classic multiplayer versus game sees you pit your mits against a huge number of opponents. Run around and swing your arm back to unleash comedic pain on your enemies – and friends – then send them flying off the map!

BEDWARS

This bizarre game is all about protecting your bed. Take on your mates to gather resources to purchase items and team upgrades. Destroy enemy beds and eliminate players to win the game!

DOODLE WORLD

Explore a mysterious island inhabited by strange creatures named Doodles! Begin your own adventure and compete against your friends to collect 10 special keys and witness the Doodles! Can you make it?

MINING SIMULATOR

Ever dreamed of spending your days underground mining? No, nor have we ... but this game makes it so much fun. Discover rare minerals before your friends and return to the surface first to collect the rewards. Can you beat them all?

BLOX FRUITS

Are you a master swordsman or a powerful blox fruit user? Train to become the strongest player ever and choose to fight your friends or have huge boss battles, sailing across the ocean to find more!

LIVETOPIA

With over four billion visits, this game is one of the most popular town-and-city games in Roblox history. Choose your own adventure with original jobs, outfits, vehicles and houses to own and enjoy!

The Good Life

Livetopia isn't just good ... it's GREAT! So many players have checked it out and keep coming back for more. You can start a life and immerse yourself in a world where you can be whoever you want and do whatever you choose!

Hardly Working

It isn't all good fun. OK, it is. Jobs are an essential part of the game and working will earn you credit for in-game purchases. You could be a pet doctor, a flight attendant, a DJ that performs gigs or even a good old-fashioned clown!

TOP TIP
Don't mind what other people have achieved. This is your world so enjoy it however you want!

Hit the Mall

There's loads to explore, from pretty countryside to sprawling cities, which are home to great shopping malls that offer you fun ways to spend your hard-earned credits. Where will you choose to go first?

Hit the Beach

All that exploring, working and shopping can be exhausting, so it's a good idea to have some chill time. Head to the beach and soak up the good weather – you can even pop into a waterpark and enjoy some thrilling rides!

Home Sweet Home

There are loads of different homes to own and enjoy. Many are free, such as the Modern House, which means you can jump straight into home ownership. There are loads of crazy fun options, such as mega tree houses, too!

GOODBYE!

What an amazing trip through Roblox this has been! Roblox is a wonderful place, full of creativity and good fun. Maybe you come to try new games each day, or perhaps you feel inspired and want to try creating your own game.

Whichever you choose, you're always at home in Roblox. Hopefully you've found some of your favourite games in these pages and you've also discovered a new experience that you didn't know about before you opened this book.

Remember, if there's a game you love, tell your friends and get them involved! The more people who play, the better many of these games will become.

See you next year!

STAYING SAFE ONLINE

YOUNGER FANS' GUIDE

Spending time online is great fun. These games might be your first experience of digital socialising, so here are a few simple rules to help you stay safe and keep the internet an awesome place to spend time:

• Never give out your real name – don't use it as your username.
• Never give out any of your personal details.

• Never tell anybody which school you go to or how old you are.
• Never tell anybody your password, except a parent or guardian.
• Before registering for any account, ask a parent or guardian for permission.
• Take regular breaks, as well as playing with parents nearby, or in shared family rooms.
• Always tell a parent or guardian if something is worrying you.

PARENTS' GUIDE

ONLINE CHAT
In most games, there is live on-screen text chat between users. Parents are advised to ensure that their children are only talking to friends and that they aren't being exposed to any adult matter.

SOUND
Sound is crucial in many video games. Players will often wear headphones, meaning parents won't be able to hear what children are listening to. Set up your console or computer to have sound coming from the TV or monitor as well as the headset, so you can hear what your child is experiencing.

REPORTING PLAYERS
If you see or hear a player being abusive, Roblox allows you to report users or interactions. You'll be able to use the Report Abuse links found throughout the site on game pages, but there may also be buttons within chat windows or game menus where you can raise a case with community managers.

SCREEN TIME
Taking regular breaks is important.
Set play sessions by using a timer.
Some games can last a long time and if your child finishes playing in the middle of a round, they could leave their teammates a player short, and lose any points they've earned. It is advisable to give an advanced warning for stopping play or clearly outlining a stopping point before any play session begins.

IN-GAME PURCHASES
Many games offer in-app purchases to enhance the game experience, but they're not required to play the game. They also don't improve a player's performance.
There are ways to set up safety measures on you child's account by setting up a PIN through Settings. Consult these before allowing your child to play any game in order to avoid any unpermitted spending on your account.